MAGIC
of
PRAYERS

Books by Lee Milteer

Feel and Grow Rich

Success is an Inside Job

Spiritual Power Tools for

Successful Selling

Reach Your Career Dreams

Walking with the Wise for Entrepreneurs

The Secrets of Peak Performance (1 and 2)

The Phenomenon: Achieve More in the Next

12 Months than the Previous 12 Years

Ultimate Entrepreneur Success Secrets

Walking with the Wise Overcoming Obstacles

Women Who Mean Business

Reclaim the Magic

The
MAGIC
of
PRAYERS

70 Powerful Prayers to
Manifest What You Desire

LEE MILTEER

RAINBOW RIDGE
BOOKS

Cover and interior design by Frame25 Productions
Cover photo © Igor Zh. c/o Shutterstock.com

Published by:
Rainbow Ridge Books, LLC
140 Rainbow Ridge Road
Faber, Virginia 22938
434-361-1723

If you are unable to order this book from your local
bookseller, you may order directly from the distributor.

Square One Publishers, Inc.
115 Herricks Road
Garden City Park, NY 11040
Phone: (516) 535-2010
Fax: (516) 535-2014
Toll-free: 877-900-BOOK

Visit the author at:
www.milteer.com
www.leemilteerschoolofwisdom.com

ISBN 978-1-937907-46-4

10 9 8 7 6 5 4 3 2

Printed on acid-free recycled paper
in the United States of America

Table of Contents

Introduction

A few years ago, I authored a book called *Spiritual Power Tools for Successful Selling*, and in the book I wrote a prayer at the end of each chapter. I received a heartfelt letter from a man who had been facing daunting legal challenges. He wrote to tell me that when he started using the prayers, they transformed him in a way he'd never expected.

He claimed that the prayers in the book healed the situation—it was completely and easily resolved without the legal battle he'd been so sure would ensue. At the end of his letter, he requested that I write an entire book of prayers.

One of my newer books, *Reclaim the Magic*, has an entire chapter on prayers. Even with an entire chapter devoted to prayer, readers kept asking for a book solely for prayers. Since I listen to what the Universe shares with me for my direction in life, I took all of these requests seriously and wrote *The Magic of Prayers* as a stand-alone book.

After I wrote the first version of *The Magic of Prayers*, I heard from a woman in Texas who used some of my prayers. She told me that she had an incredibly dysfunctional family . . . there was always chaos, anger, frustration, and retaliation. Family events were miserable for everyone involved. Even though she wasn't sure they would work, she was at her wit's end and started using several of my prayers every day to heal her family. Within three months, she discovered that the prayers actually worked on her family. Because she was so determined to heal the family and use the prayers every day, something shifted inside of her. She was more at peace with her family. She became more loving and forgiving and because she changed, everyone in her family shifted as well. As a family, their behaviors changed and they became (and still are today) a more positive and loving family. She learned that all things can be healed and observed that when you make changes to your internal world, the outer world will follow suit.

A mother named Kelli wrote to tell me that her teenage son had fallen in with the wrong crowd. His grades plummeted and the sweet child she knew turned into an angry teenager who was hostile and verbally abusive. She used the prayers from *Reclaim the Magic* twice a day to find a healing place where she and her son could move back into harmony. She said it took her about two months before she saw improvement, but she kept going with the inner prayer work. To her surprise, her son's behaviors changed. He stopped hanging out with negative and destructive peers and started to study and get good grades again. Right now, he's working hard in school and is applying to get in to some impressive universities. Kelli said that she believed with her entire heart that the prayers were the solution to the problem.

I do believe that concealed within any problem or challenge is an opportunity for spiritual growth that results in greater understanding and opens us to new energy. The truth is, if there's a problem, there is also an answer. No problem is too great to place in Infinite Intelligence's hands.

We must believe that in prayer, the Creator has entrusted us with a force that can move the Heavenly world and bring its power down to us on earth. Prayer is the difference between the best you can do and the best GOD CAN DO. When we pray, we shift the center of living from self-consciousness to self-surrender because prayer is the secret of power. The power of prayer opens mental prisons and dissolves the chains that bind you to your problems. Be open to the Creator's wisdom, for it is a gift that blesses you and those for whom you pray.

When I sat down to write *The Magic of Prayers*, Infinite Intelligence flowed through me. The prayers in this book flowed to me from a much higher source than myself, and I am honored to be able to share them with you. You'll find that this book contains prayers that are practical, concise, and easy to read, which will help you feel connected to the Creator and allow answers to flow to you.

When you pray, unexpected things happen because you cannot limit the Creator's powers. Prayer is the key that unlocks all doors. Your job is to pray, trust God, let go, and wait for the will of heaven to give you inspiration to take action. There are no problems too great to place in the Creator's hands. All things are possible through spirit.

Blessings, Love, and Magic to you.

Lee Milteer
Leemilteerschoolofwisdom.com

The Magic of Prayers

The absolute truth is that prayer can and will create magic in your life. The first thing that you must understand and believe is that you are capable of being in connection with Infinite Intelligence. Think of prayer as a form of therapy to help you avoid struggle and strain. Infinite Intelligence has the ability and all the wisdom and power necessary to solve any of your problems.

You do not need to have any willpower or muscle power because praying is a mental and spiritual therapeutic technique. When you pray, you are enacting spiritual law. Infinite Intelligence is an "indwelling presence" and your prayers connect your consciousness with that Divine presence.

When you pray, you commune with Infinite Intelligence; you sense it and feel it. The approach to Infinite Intelligence is direct—through your own consciousness. The Infinite Intelligence is all-knowing, all-powerful, and omnipresent, within every atom of the universe, including us. When we pray, we set in motion the ever-mysterious forces that bring the answers we seek.

As the Bible promises, "Ask and it shall be given you; seek and ye shall find; knock and the door shall be opened." When you ask, be sure to clearly define your desires. It is difficult for Infinite Intelligence to give you innovative ideas, directions, or answers to create the life you want for yourself if you are not clear and specific about your desires. This small book will assist you to connect to Divine Intelligence with powerful prayers that address your requests.

The Bible also tells us, "Before they call will I answer." When you pray, you become in vibrational harmony with the answer you are seeking and in that way attract it to yourself. So the act of praying—that is, thanking Infinite Intelligence in advance for solutions and intuitive insight— attracts the results you want in your life by matching vibration levels with an inspired solution.

Prayer is often said to be a mental approach to the reality of spirit. We pray to demonstrate an invisible law that has power over the visible and it is often said that great manifesting begins with learning to pray. Every day it would benefit you to take the time to pray for yourself and others. Great spiritual masters have suggested that we should always pray as we awake and pray as we go to sleep. These prayers connect us to Infinite Intelligence and help open the door to our inner wisdom.

By thanking your God Source in prayer before you actually receive the blessings you desire, you are accepting your good in the present moment. This works because energetically speaking, there is only now. You are a co-creator with the Infinite Intelligence. Trust that it hears you loud and clear and will start to deliver your desires to you in ways you never could have dreamed.

When you declare your intentions to Infinite Intelligence through prayer, you open the way for them to manifest and appear in your life. Once you have prayed for someone or about something that you need answers for, be observant and aware, and allow the world to answer you. Your answers may come in a book, a song, a conversation with someone else, a movie, or a television show. As they say, God works in mysterious ways, so be open for messages.

You can pray for wisdom and harmony, or pray to send healing to the world or to yourself. I have always prayed for all the people in my life, both personally and in my business. It keeps me connected to my purpose in this life.

Tips for Effective Prayers

In my research and through personal experience with prayer, I have found that when you put a group of like-minded people together who are attuned to the same goal, results from prayer seem to come faster. A Christian bible verse speaks of this principle: Matthew 18:20.

> *"For where two or three are gathered together in my name, there am I in the midst of them."*

Another important aspect of prayer is to always remember that you are an instrument of the light. Your words are not as powerful as your feelings when you pray. Remember that you are in a vibrational universe and feelings generate a stronger vibration to your mental image. You must literally create vibration when you pray, not just mouth the words of unfelt prayers. Prayer uses your conscious mind and then transfers that vibration (information) to your subconscious mind, to be connected to the Infinite Intelligence.

The truth is that you can pray for anything you want . . . but unless you are a vibrational (emotional) match to that request, the prayer cannot manifest. We live in a perfect universe and its own law of attraction governs it. The Universe cannot deliver something to you that you're not in vibrational harmony with, or that you're not ready to receive. Further, it cannot deliver a blessing to someone for whom you pray, if that person is not a vibrational match to your prayer.

Prayers do not have to be long. Normally when you try to pray for a long time, it means you are trying to force things by using mental coercion, which always results in the opposite of what you are praying for. In my research, I have found that short prayers said from the heart get better results than long prayers. You will know when you can stop praying for something when you feel a sense of peace and well-being. Expect your prayers for wholeness, vitality, abundance, and peace to be answered. Be sure you let go and relax after praying because doing so will allow you to stay aligned with your intent and receive the answers you seek.

Once you have completed your prayers, you sincerely need to know and believe they have been heard. Amen means, "So be it." Thank Infinite Intelligence and from that point forward, consider the matter to be closed or resolved. If you want results, you must not waver. To waver is to doubt and to doubt is to not believe. All of your prayers are a waste of energy if you do not believe. If you do not truly feel it is possible for your prayers to be answered, I guarantee you it is not.

Prayers for You

You may use these Prayers as stated or you can rewrite and customize them for your own situation, needs, and desires. To get the best results, you must FEEL yourself connect with Infinite Intelligence, be present, and honestly and sincerely communicate your needs. You can phrase your requests to God, Infinite Intelligence, Source, Spirit, Universe, or any other term that makes you feel spiritually connected with all there is.

Carry this book with you in your pocket, purse, or briefcase to be inspired to take spiritual action first before physical action.

God's To-Do List

Make a list of things that you would like the Infinite Intelligence to act upon. Include anything you are unable to act on immediately, either because you don't know how to get started, or don't have the time or resources to support it. These are very important prayers. This is important to do, so you can clearly identify your desires. This exercise allows you to set an intention and then let Infinite Intelligence handle the details of bringing it to you. The Infinite Intelligence has the ability to arrange details and circumstances much better than you.

Your job is to specifically define what it is you want, envision it clearly, and then be alert enough to see it when it presents itself to you! Infinite Intelligence will handle bringing you the knowledge, people, and opportunities necessary to accomplish your goals.

You will get assistance through intuition, gut feelings, knowing, and inspiration. You must acknowledge the inspiration and follow through on what your intuition tells you to do next. Then and only then should you take inspired action. The old saying, "God helps those who help themselves," is true.

By getting clear about what you want to happen during your day, you will be ready to see the opportunities when they are presented to you.

In case you have never done a God's To-Do List, the following are a few suggestions you can use to get started. Add your own details to each of the items. It's important that you write out what you really want and need from Infinite Intelligence.

Dear Infinite Intelligence . . .
Please give me the ability to see the good in
others so they can see the good in me.

Dear Infinite Intelligence . . .
Please give me the ability to move past all

negative thinking, help me to remove grudges,
and stop feeling like a victim. Please open my
mind and heart to more peace and love.

Dear Infinite Intelligence . . .
Please bring me the situations, opportunities,
and the people that will bring great
prosperity to my family and me.

Dear Infinite Intelligence . . .
Please open my eyes to the wonderful blessings
I now have, and let me be filled with more
gratitude and appreciation every day.

Dear Infinite Intelligence . . .
Please inspire me to make better choices with
food, drink, and exercise for a healthy, strong
body that is filled with vitality.

Dear Infinite Intelligence . . .
Please inspire me to attract a new job, find a
better place to live, improve my relationships,
etc. (Add the details of how you'd like each of
these to unfold.)

Now you have to trust that Infinite Intelligence will hear you loud and clear and will start to deliver your desires to you in known and unknown ways. Because you took the time to be clear about what you wanted, you'll recognize the opportunities as they come to you and be ready to take action on your desires.

I want to remind you that you must ask for help through heartfelt Prayers before it is delivered . . . because your spiritual helpers must honor your free will. You live in a "free-will" world, which means you can choose positive realities or negative realities. Infinite Intelligence is not going to assist or give information without it being requested. Your real job is to establish your awareness of your partnership with your God Source, then create the habits and rituals that will build a great life for you.

You can reclaim the magic of being connected to Infinite Intelligence, but you have to make the first move! All of these blessings from prayers will happen when you take the time to join forces with your God Source to pave the way before you. Experiment with the use of prayers in your life and I am sure you will enjoy the results.

The Prayers

Prayer for Attracting
New Friends

Infinite Intelligence:
I call upon you and The Divine Love Source
to now easily and effortlessly attract new
people into my life circles. I now only attract
people who are uplifting,
fun, joyful, intelligent, spiritual, generous,
trustworthy, who share interests,
and are compatible to me. I now attract
people, events, and organizations
that I find mentally and spiritually
stimulating and rewarding.
I release the victim part of me that held me
back from meeting new people.
I release past hurt and open my heart to a
future that is filled with people
who truly belong in my community
and who are aligned with me.

I am grateful to have the opportunity
to meet and learn from new people.
I will never feel lonely because I
know that Infinite Intelligence has
the perfect people lined up to meet me
when my heart is open to this new
reality of attracting friends.
Thank you for all the connections
to the adventurous souls who
open my mind and spirit to
new knowledge and joyful adventures.
Thank you for bringing wonderfully fun
and enthusiastic souls into my life circle.
Thank you for allowing us to make
a mutually beneficial contribution
to each other's lives.
Thank you for the wisdom
and support I get from these
wonderful, long-term friends.
It is a win-win for all concerned.
So be it.

Thank you. Amen.

Prayer to Awaken
Your Authentic Self

Dear Source:
I ask you to assist me in updating my
authentic self-knowledge, my connection
to you, my knowledge that I'm a
perfect child of the universe.
Please remove the old programmed
self-image that society has imprinted on me.
Give me the insight and wisdom of
knowing that I'm a manifestor and creator.
I am connected to a powerful spirit source
and all my needs and answers come from
within; I need not look to the
outside for guidance.
Give me the courage and the
strength to access information
to form the inner intuitive part of

myself and not rely on the latest
trends from the outside world.
The God Source is my supply
and answers all of my challenges.
I give myself permission to truly treat
myself with love, respect, and honor.
I give myself permission to be unique,
original, and authentic, regardless
of what others think, say, or do.
My connection is with spirit.
I am one with the Infinite
Intelligence and I source my
answers from inner knowing.
So be it.

Thank you. Amen.

Prayer for Balance

Dear Infinite Intelligence:
I know when things are out of balance that
my life and affairs are seeking a new reality.
I know that my highest and best good will
come into being with my faith and my
connection to the Infinite Intelligence.
I know that to be disturbed about one's
life and affairs even for an instant
is not to trust the Divine Love that is
gifted to me daily by the God Source.
I know I will be guided into a
balanced state of mind and affairs.
Infinite Intelligence is taking care of me
and I trust this loving care in all that I do.
If my outer world is out of balance,
I am not disturbed because I am one with
the love of the Infinite Intelligence.

I know that with my spiritual helpers,
I can shift my energy into balance.
Thank you, Infinite Intelligence, for
your steady presence and guidance
to always bring my personal life
and work life into balance.
Thank you for inspiring me to create
boundaries for my time and life energy.
Thank you for your support to easily and
gracefully release relationships and
situations that are no longer beneficial for me.
Thank you for helping me set my priorities in
order. Thank you for removing confusion,
hesitation, frustration, and all negative
emotions that kept me from declaring love
and balance in all aspects of my life.
All is well. So be it.

Thank you. Amen.

PRAYER TO BE
A GOOD PARENT

Dear Creator:
Thank you for the gift of being a parent.
Help me to see and keep my focus
today on the blessings, gifts, and joys of
being the parent of my precious children.
Thank you for giving me grace and please
take away past guilt, pain, regrets, and
suffering. Please take away my troubles
and allow peace and tranquility in my
life so that my child can know truth
and connection to the Divine.
Give me the strength to be conscious
of my life and how my example will
imprint upon my children's view of reality.
Please remove any victimhood mentality,
grudges, and negative attitudes I have

so that my innocent children are not
saddled with this heavy energy.
Please help me be kind, patient, gentle,
and loving, slow to anger, and fast to
forgiveness. Allow me to be filled with
gratitude and joy every day.
Please help me to remember the power
of my attitude and words on my family's
hearts. Give me the mental, physical,
emotional, spiritual, and financial support
that I need daily to be a good
role model and parent.
Thank you for the gifts I learn daily
from my children. I declare that we,
as a family, will always be close, loving,
and good to each other.
We are a loving family. So be it.

Thank you. Amen.

Prayer to Be of Service

Dear Spirit:
Please give me the insight and
perception to rise above the
Mundane and use my talents,
experience, and abilities to
share love in the world with
my actions and thoughts.
Give my life a sense of purpose and joy.
Use me as an instrument of light
for you in the world with every soul I
encounter. I surrender my job to you.
Assist me to remember that my real job
is to be of service and to send positive
energy into the world. And so it is.

Thank you. Amen.

PRAYER FOR BLESSED OPPORTUNITIES

Dear Universe:
Thank you for opening my eyes, ears, mind,
and heart to know and recognize blessed
opportunities. Thank you for my creative
and visionary abilities to clearly see new
options to take that will bring me health,
happiness, prosperity, and success.
I trust the Universe's guidance.
My life becomes more rewarding and blessed
daily. I now take ACTION on my Divine
Inspiration to use my talents, skills,
and knowledge in new and exciting ways.
Everything I want and need flows to me now.
I intend to flow with Universal Energy
of love and harmony.
Good things always come to me.

I live joyously, spontaneously, and
enthusiastically, for the Universe is always
expressing through me in all my affairs.
I am blessed. So be it.

Thank you. Amen.

PRAYER FOR
BUSINESS CLIENTS

Dear Spirit:
The peace and love of Infinite Intelligence
fills my soul and entire being.
I am illumined and healing love flows
from me to all my clients.
Divine love operates in and
through my business daily.
Infinite Intelligence's love and blessings
are offered to all those who do business
with me and work with me.
I am grateful for the countless blessings
that flow to my business and for my
clients every day. So be it.

Thank you. Amen.

PRAYER FOR
BUSINESS SUCCESS

Dear God Source:
I bless my business because it is God's
business. I offer thoughts of prosperity,
abundance, and the best service to
everyone I deal with daily.
Everything I need is drawn to me though
God's sources. Customers, clients,
ideas, solutions, and prosperity
come to me easily and effortlessly.
I bless all my transactions
and the people I work with.
Love permeates all of my business dealings.
My business is God's business and God's
divine energy leads me to success.
I am in partnership with God; I cannot fail.
God is my supply. And so it is.

Thank you. Amen.

Prayer for Clarity

Dear God:
In the clear bright light of Divine Truth,
there is no darkness, confusion, or
overwhelm. Nothing troubles me.
I cast all my burdens, anxiety, and confusion
on to the Divine Source of all Love.
Love is the law of life. I sow love into
all that I do and think and feel.
Where there is confusion or feelings
of overwhelm, I cast these mental
troubles unto the Infinite Intelligence and
know that I can release my worries.
I am transformed into peace.
Please reveal yourself to me in new ways
today. Fill my heart with your comfort.
Fill my body and mind with your strength.
Help me trade my confusion, worry, and

stress for peace and order in my life.
I allow the Divine Energy of love to guide
me daily and I dwell in the kingdom of
harmony and order. I bring love and
peace wherever I go.
All is well in my world and
I am open to heavenly inspiration
and guidance for seeing new solutions.
So be it.

Thank you. Amen.

Prayer for Clear
Desires & Intentions

Dear Infinite Intelligence:
In this moment I know that I
am a positive, powerful being,
clear on my desires and
purposeful in my intentions.
The universe and my body
and mind arrange for me to receive
my every need and desire, and
they come to me in wonderful ways.
And so it is.

Thank you. Amen.

PRAYER FOR COLLECTING MONEY OWED

Dear Infinite Intelligence:
All things are part of Infinite Intelligence
and money is part of that reality.
God grant me the ease of collecting
monies that are owed to me.
There is fair exchange for value. I have
provided the value and I ask the Universe
now to assist me in regaining the balance of
all things by being paid. I pray for Divine ease
and speed in collecting my fair
and rightfully due payments.
I send love and appreciation to those
who owe me money and I ask Infinite
Intelligence to assist them to be honorable
and prosperous. Allow them to easily,
effortlessly, and happily pay the

debts they owe on time.
I ask that they are assisted with
blessings of prosperity so that
whatever they pay me comes back
to them easily and effortlessly.
Thank you, Infinite Intelligence.
All monies that are due to me are now paid
with ease and peace. All is well.
So be it.

Thank you. Amen.

PRAYER FOR COURAGE

Dear Divine Spirit:
I am always safe and loved, and when
acting from inspiration, will always
be taken care of in this world.
I am asking for courage right now
to do the thing I know in my heart
I need to do. I call upon your love to instill
into my heart the right energy pattern
so that I clearly see the path I must take.
I ask for courage to easily take the path
that is to my highest and best good.
Assist me to release the victim energy
that holds me back from accessing
the powerful free spirit that is within me.
Give me courage to fly and be free
of the past and all its limiting believes
and powers over me. I unite with you,

Dear Spirit, and feel my life force
merge with yours. I am one with you.
Thank you for helping me see exactly
what is going on in my life and helping
me confidently know that I will step
forward into the unknown and be
safe and protected by spirit.
I open my heart and mind to new
solutions to deal with my earthy challenges.
I never give up because I know I am in the
process of always becoming.
I refuse to allow destructive thoughts,
lack, despair, discouragement, or
any type of limitations to have a
place in my world or consciousness.
Outer conditions have no power over me.
I claim connection to all that is Divine Spirit.
So be it.

Thank you. Amen.

Prayer for
Creating Harmony

Mother, Father, Guardian of the Universe:
I ask you to hold me and all those souls
who I have conflict or difficulty with
in your light. I ask that you now heal
unharmonious relationships forever
and create permanent goodwill.
Give me the strength to see the
good in others and give them
the strength to see the good in me.
Allow my positive thoughts and my love
and prayers for these people to
embody them. Inspire our interactions
to be joyful and harmonious. So be it.

Thank you. Amen.

PRAYER FOR CREATIVE ENERGY & SPIRIT

Dear Source:
Inspire me to allow my authentic creative
spirit to come out to play and create.
Remove perfectionism, judgment,
and comparison energy from me.
Mute the critic within me so I can allow
myself to join in the flow of Universal love
energy that is our creative spirit.
Assist me to hear your Divine Guidance.
Direct me to use my life energy in the most
creative, productive, profitable, and
spirit-directed ways possible. Give me
confidence and faith that I am
connected to you and all of light.
I know that I am always under the direct
inspiration of Infinite Intelligence

for all my creative endeavors.
My work is God's work. I easily and
effortlessly make right decisions. So be it.

Thank you. Amen.

PRAYER FOR DEALING
WITH DIFFICULT PEOPLE

Dear Source:
All that I do today and every day
is centered in harmony and peace.
I am a light worker and I spread only
light in the world. Everywhere I go,
I take my peace and harmony with me.
Nothing from the outside world can disturb
me for I am one with the Cosmic Harmony.
I accept people can only do as
well as they know how to do.
Where I see discord I sow only love
and say "Peace Be Still."
I release bitterness and resentment
and only offer love and light. I easily
walk away from dissension and discord
and accept that I do not have to see life

from only my perspective.
People have the right to create
Whatever drama they wish and
I do not have to participate.
The harmony within me radiates
to everyone and all situations I am in.
I am a peacemaker in life and I always
give myself permission to forgive
and let others go on their own path.
It is not my job to fix them.
It is only my job to bring love and
light into the world. So be it.

Thank you. Amen.

Prayer for Dealing with Jealousy & Envy

Dear Universe:
There is no place for troublesome
people in my life. I rejoice at the
good fortune of another. I love to
see others excel at whatever they do.
I recognize that the Christ within me
is in the Christ within you.
I am now automatically dissolving
any thoughts of discord in my
consciousness and yours. I understand
and accept that each person
in my life is expressing God at his
own level of awareness.
I am at peace with the world.
The peace of God is in my peace
for I am part of the Divine Intelligence.

No one can hurt me unless I let them hurt
me. Conditions have no power over me.
I am one with the God Source.
Where there appears to be troubled waters,
I say "peace be still." Where there is
dissension and discord, I sow love.
I am now releasing jealousy and envy to
Divine Intelligence. So be it.

Thank you. Amen.

PRAYER FOR DEALING
WITH LEGAL TROUBLES

Dear Infinite Intelligence:
Please supply me with the strength and
courage to stand in my truth during any
legal proceedings. I invite your intervention
of love and healing energy to solve
and dissolve these legal challenges.
Please remove all negative emotions
such as conflict, fear, anger,
retribution, and retaliation.
Give me the patience and fortitude
to hold my tongue, calm my emotions,
and temper my reactions. I strive
to think and act with a calm connection
to Infinite Intelligence. I pray for all disputes
to end quickly and amicably. Everyone finds
a mutually acceptable compromise to avoid

pursuing the case in court.
The Infinite Intelligence that is within me
and my team is also in the opposition team.
Disputes between all parties
are now healed and forgiven.
I pray for my happiness in life to be
multiplied. I pray for the emotional
and spiritual self of all parties
concerned to be restored.
Time heals all wounds and
this wound heals quickly.
Thank you, Infinite Intelligence for
your intervention in this situation.
Thank you for creating a releasing and
healing, so all parties can go on with their
lives with more happiness, joy, and harmony.
So be it.

Thank you. Amen.

PRAYER OF DETACHMENT

Dear Source:
I am at peace. I am God's perfect Child.
I don't take anything personally. I am
undisturbed. I believe in the power of God in
my life and there is no power in conditions or
personalities unless I give them power.
Nothing can upset or disturb me.
I feel nothing done against me.
I allow all souls to be on their own path
and learn their own lessons. I give them
permission to have their own opinions.
Nothing in my past or future can hurt me.
I trust the Divine Law of Life to take care of
all my needs. I now trust the Infinite
Wisdom of God working in and through me
to bring me my good. I am undisturbed and
always at peace. And so it is.

Thank you. Amen.

PRAYER FOR DIRECTION

Dear Infinite Intelligence:
Guide me to a renewal of spirit. Open my
heart and mind to receive from you a new
message of direction for my highest
and best good and for the good of all.
I trust that God will provide me with the
ideas, motivation, and clarity for
my highest and best manifestation.
I can do anything through my love and
connection to the God Source.
The same Infinite Intelligence that holds the
stars in their courses and maintains the whole
universe in perfect balance keeps
me in my perfect balance now.
I dwell in the security that my needs
are met and that my circumstances are
maintained in perfect balance with the

harmonious whole of life. Order is the
first rule of heaven and my life is filled
with peace, joy, love, and prosperity.
My needs are always met with love.
Love and light always guide me
in all that I do. So be it.

Thank you. Amen.

PRAYER FOR
DIVINE INSPIRATION

Dear Infinite Intelligence,
I come to you humble for I do not have
all the answers. I call upon you to hear
my request for Divine Inspiration on
how to handle my challenges and goals.
I am willing to put aside my ego and
the need to be right and open myself
to Divine Inspiration for all the
answers to my needs and desires.
I know that all I have to do is ASK
and be willing to listen and my
answers will come to me through
other people, books, movies, and
other earthily ways. I ask you for the
inspiration to be clear and direct to me
with grace, gentleness, and love, so

that I can easily follow your guidance.
I am willing to ask and wait for divine
inspiration before I take hasty actions
or reactions. I am confident of my
connection to spirit and that my
personal requests will be answered.
I know that all is well in my world
when I am connected to you.
Thank you in advance for the love,
connections, and direction from you.
I am always assured success by
taking action after Divine Inspiration.
So be it.

Thank you. Amen.

PRAYER FOR DIVINE TIME

Dear Infinite Intelligence,
When I am delayed I know I am being
protected and that all is well.
There is no power in conditions.
Give me the wisdom to use my time wisely.
Assist me to recognize people, situations,
and circumstances that rob me of my
precious time. Allow me to say no
with love to anything that wastes my
time or depletes me from my
creative purpose on earth.
Give me the strength to have
boundaries with my time and
life's resources so I can focus my
attention on the people and things
that are really important to me
and my life's purpose.

Assist me to have patience with myself,
know that I am always connected
to Infinite Intelligence, and to listen
to my intuition about the best use of
my time and life energy. I am one with
Infinite Intelligence and all is well.
The right ideas, people, and situations
show up for me at the perfect time
because I am always connected to
my source and listening for guidance.
I declare divine time in my life.
Everything I need always flows
to me at the perfect time. So be it.

Thank you. Amen.

PRAYER FOR
EMOTIONAL PROTECTION

Dear Divine Intelligence:
I am now releasing all my problems and
fears to the Divine Infinite Intelligence.
I forgive all those who have hurt me.
I bless them in their onward journey.
I forgive myself for the part
I played in any problems.
I trust in the Divine Intelligence
to protect me, and those that I love.
I face the future with glad assurance
and peace. I am always protected.
I am forever in harmony with
the truth that sets me free. So be it.

Thank you. Amen.

PRAYER TO ENHANCE
YOUR LIFE PURPOSE

Dear Universe:
Assist me today to delicately
guide my thoughts and images
in my mind's eye to thoughts
of peace, harmony, perfect health,
happiness, prosperity,
and well-being in my life.
Allow me to see myself as confident,
filled with vitality and good health,
and enthusiastic about my life and work.
Allow me to work out any "problems"
in my mind and to see the perfect
solutions as they come to me.
Thank you for your guidance
and creative new solutions to fulfill
my life's purpose. And so it is.

Thank you. Amen.

Prayer for Finding the Perfect Animal Companion (Pet)

Infinite Intelligence:
You are all there is and
are connected to everything.
I know there is a perfect animal
companion (pet) waiting
for me to find them.
I ask Divine Cosmic Love Energy
to arrange circumstances where I
and my new animal companion
are easily connected.
I ask for patience, open heart energy,
and Divine Inspiration to know
the right connection and
to know when to take action.
I ask for the best information and

knowledge to know what this specific
animal companion needs to thrive.
I accept that my animal companion
(pet) has a unique spirit and has come
to Earth to live its own reincarnation.
I accept that my animal companion
was born to experience their own calling
and I am part of their choice.
I will love and nurture my animal's
spirit as well as their body.
Thank you, Creator, for the gift of their
presence in my life. And so it is.

Thank you. Amen.

Prayer for Finding the Perfect Renter

Infinite Intelligence:
You are all there is and
are connected to everything.
I am asking for the perfect renter,
who meets all the criteria I require
to thrive in my rental unit.
I ask Divine Cosmic Love Energy
to arrange circumstances where I and
my perfect renter are easily connected.
I ask for Divine Inspiration to know
the right renter and to know when
to take action. I ask for the best
information and knowledge
to understand what this specific
perfect renter needs to thrive.
Thank you, Infinite Intelligence,

for a perfectly matched renter,
who always pays on time, is
respectful and protective over
the rental unit, is quiet and considerate,
and is easy to do business with.
Thank you, Creator, for the gift
of their presence in my life.
Thank you for allowing this to be
a positive relationship for both parties.
So be it.

Thank you. Amen.

Prayer for Finding
the Perfect Roommate

Dear Universe:
I ask for your assistance to attract the
roommate who is best suited to me now.
Infinite Intelligence is connected to
everything and I choose to attract
a person who meets all the qualifications
I require so we both thrive as roommates.
Please arrange a living situation
that is a win-win for all concerned.
I ask Divine Cosmic Love Energy
to arrange circumstances where I and my
perfect roommate are easily connected.
I ask for Divine Inspiration to know
the right connection and to know
when to take action.
I ask for this new environment

to allow us all to thrive.
Thank you, Infinite Intelligence, for
a perfectly matched roommate who
pays on time, is respectful and
appreciative, is quiet and considerate,
and is easy to live with.
Thank you, Creator, for the gift
of their presence in my life
and allowing it to be a positive
relationship for both parties. So be it.

Thank you. Amen.

PRAYER FOR FITNESS
MOTIVATION

Dear Creator:
I ask for your grace and love to assist me
in exercising and moving my body in
positive ways that benefit my long-term
wellbeing. Inspire me to engage in a
physically active life to enhance my
mental and physical health.
I accept my body-mind connection
and appreciate that taking care of my
body is also a spiritual habit.
As of today, I honor my body
and nurture it with walks, dancing,
swimming, and any other form of movement
that rejuvenates my body and spirit.
Everything I need to achieve this new
movement and exercise is drawn to me

through Creator's sources.
Thank you, spirit, for putting
the fun back into movement.
I choose activities that are
effective and enjoyable.
I love variety in my movements and
I allow myself to be a connection
to the Creator when I am
in the flow of movement.
Life is a beautiful dance
and I now love moving with life
and channeling love energy to myself
through my physical movements.
I am in partnership with The Creator
and I cannot fail. I tune into the
movement energy that the Creator
is flowing all the time. So be it.

Thank you. Amen.

PRAYER FOR
FORGIVENESS OF OTHERS

Dear Infinite Intelligence:
I forgive and release all those who
have ever hurt or offended me.
I now forgive them totally and completely.
Forgiveness opens the door to
Divine right action in my reality.
The Christ Consciousness within me
works with the Christ Consciousness
within them and all things are healed
and forgiven. So be it.

Thank you. Amen.

PRAYER FOR
FORGIVENESS OF SELF

Dear Infinite Intelligence:
I forgive myself for all my past mistakes.
I release all condemnation.
I release all destructive feelings
about my past mistakes.
I freely let go of the past.
I am now a better person
every day in every way.
I am one with Infinite Intelligence
and I am free. So be it.

Thank you. Amen.

Prayer for Getting Unstuck

Infinite intelligence:
I cast my burden of feeling stuck
upon you and trust that the right
inspiration will come to me.
I am always at the right place
at the right time.
I am willing to let go of my
limited mindset and open my mind to
unlimited potential of what is possible.
I joyfully shift my energy to open my
mind, my heart, and my soul to the callings
of my deep inner connection to spirit.
I trust in the divine law of life with all my
heart, knowing as I accept nothing but
good, all things work together for good
through the Infinite Intelligence. So be it.

Thank you. Amen.

Prayer for
Goal-Driven Behavior

Dear God:
I am now one with Source.
Infinite Intelligence is filling me
with the power to define, clarify,
and carry through with exactly
the right and perfect goals for my life.
I now pursue only those goals about
Which I have received clarity and
direction from Infinite Intelligence.
With Infinite Intelligence as my partner,
I have all the energy, focus, and right ideas
I need to succeed in my goals. So be it.

Thank you. Amen.

PRAYER FOR GUIDANCE

Dear Universe:
Please assist me to hear
your Divine Guidance.
Direct me to use my life
energy in the most productive,
profitable, and spirit-directed ways.
Give me confidence and faith to know
that I am connected to you and to all life.
I know that I am always under the
direct inspiration of Infinite Intelligence.
I make right decisions
easily and effortlessly. So be it.

Thank you. Amen.

Prayer for Happiness

Dear Universe:
Inspire me to see my reality with
fresh new eyes and focus on the amazing
blessings I have right now in my life,
work, relationships, and health.
Open the inner doors of insight
and intuition that allow me to truly
be in the moment and presence of the
miracles that are surrounding me daily.
Please awaken me to view life with more
patience, understanding, and compassion
towards myself and others.
Give me the awareness to recognize
my perfectionist expectations
and let them go with ease.
I open the connection to Divine Spirit
within myself and the connection

to all there is. Ignite within me great
gratitude for all the blessings
in my life and all those
who have supported me.
Motivate me to see and enjoy all
the amazing opportunities
to be happy every day.
Open my heart to being happy
regardless of circumstances so I can be
a light into the world and illuminate
a path for others. So be it.

Thank you. Amen.

PRAYER TO HEAL ILLNESS

Dear Lord:
I call upon you now and always
in times of weakness and need to be
connected with you. I accept as fact
that I have the power to help heal myself
with my connection to spirit.
I can see that an illness or dis-ease
is out of alignment with source.
I can choose right now to be proactive
about my spiritual connection and
my mind, body, and soul connection.
I ask to be your servant of
Divine Earth Light at this time.
I know that I am one with you
and I am always connected and safe.
I willingly release all negative thoughts
and know that I will actively release

the old energy of the illness that is
getting my attention. I now renew my
life with you as my guide for health and
recovery. Thank you, Lord, for
strength to not blame or shame myself
for the history that created this temporary
bodily situation. I choose to connect with
spirit and allow the power of the Divine to
flow through me at all times. I give myself
permission to totally shift my energy flow
and create a new healthy reality.
I forgive myself and all others who
I have had negative thoughts towards.
I allow the light of the God Force to enter
all of my energy fields and fill
me with Divine Love Energy.
I accept that the Divine Love
has the ability to transform
and transmute all past energy
and create new energy flows that
lead to health and vitality in my life.

I am always creating myself and am
never stuck in old or past circumstances.
My point of power is right now connected
to the Source and all that I need flows
to me easily and effortlessly.
I call upon Divine Healing in my
Life now from all the helpers of
my health and wellbeing. So be it.

Thank you. Amen.

PRAYER TO
HEAL LONELINESS

Dear Source:
I am the perfect child of the
Universe and I am never alone.
There is a divine love around me at all
times. I am loved, I am safe, and I am always
connected to my spirit guides,
my higher self, and my soul's purpose.
Everything that I need is provided to me
when I align with the Cosmic Love
Energy because I am God in action.
Infinite Intelligence guides me daily
towards those on Earth who are
for my highest and best good.
I am never alone. I always have a
team of invisible helpers who hear
my every prayer and wish, and
through my intuition, guide me
to my highest and best good.

I am now surrounding myself with
self-love and the love of the Divine God.
I am now easily and effortlessly
attracting wonderful companions
who love and appreciate me
and who support and comfort me.
I am guided to be at the right place
at the right time in the world to meet new
perfect people who I will feel connected to.
Daily, I am opening my heart and mind
to attract new people who enhance
my reality as I enhance theirs.
I now devote my life to be a
messenger of love for Earth.
I am the perfect child of the universe
and I am never alone.
I see the God source in all others
and they see the God source in me.
All is in divine harmony
and peace in my life.
I rejoice daily on my blessings.
And so it is.

Thank you. Amen.

PRAYER FOR HEALTH

Dear Universe:
I know that it is your will
that I have good health.
I now only think thoughts of
health, vitality, and faith.
I give no power to symptoms
or conditions of dis-ease.
Infinite Intelligence supplies
me with all that I need and
I see myself as whole and healthy.
I am love and light.
I am whole and my body
and mind are restored.
I am a divine, perfect, spiritual
being, forever with Infinite Intelligence.
So be it.

Thank you. Amen.

PRAYER FOR INTUITION

Dear God Source:
I know I am always under
your direct inspiration.
There are no mysteries in God's kingdom
and whatever I should know will now be
revealed to me with grace and ease.
I am a perfect instrument and can bring
my perfect good into the world
in perfect ways.
Knowing this is true, I listen
in the silence and know exactly
what to do in all circumstances.
I am connected with you and
my intuition is the instrument that
allows me to hear and connect with you.
And so it is.

Thank you. Amen.

PRAYER FOR JOY

Dear Spirit:
Help me to take myself lightly
so that I may play with the angels.
I know that I bring the power of joy
into my relationships and into
each day and every environment.
Thank you for reminding me to
be "light" on my feet! So be it.

Thank you. Amen.

PRAYER FOR MAKING
GOOD DECISIONS

Infinite Intelligence:
Please inspire me to connect with you to
gather facts and then wait at least 24 hours
to allow my brain to digest information
before I make an important decision.
I will listen to the still, small voice
within me and be guided to make
the best and right decision.
I will be aware of the influence
and pressure of others, as well as
their agendas for requests for
my time, money, or resources.
I give myself permission for all
decisions to be beneficial for me
and everyone involved.
I allow myself the time and space

I need to make the right decision.
I am immune to pressure since
I am partners with Divine Intelligence.
I know there is a perfect solution to
every situation and being connected to
my Source, I will at all times be guided
to the highest and best decisions. So be it.

Thank you. Amen.

Prayer for Miracles

Dear Universe:
I call upon you right now to bring to me
a miracle to change my circumstances.
Give me the insight and intuition
daily to follow your lead.
Motivate me daily to be open-minded
and curious and take inspired
to achieve my miracles.
I ask that new energy is sent to me
to heal, harmonize, and balance my entire
being and all circumstances of my life.
All the resources I need to do my work on
Earth are being drawn to me now.
I am magnetic, and I accept
miracles in my life now.
Let love, light, prosperity, and good
health always protect me in all travels

and worldly endeavors. Bless my
life, home, family, and work daily.
Thank you for the whispers of intuition,
the guidance of good people, and
the signals I receive from the Universe,
for these direct me toward the highest
and best for my life and soul purpose.
I am so thankful for the small
and large miracles of my life daily.
I have so much to be grateful for.
I am connected to the Universe and
I am always protected and loved.
So be it.

Thank you. Amen.

Prayer for Motivation

Dear Infinite Intelligence:
Guide me to a renewal of spirit and
motivation in my life and work.
Open my heart and mind to receive
from you a new message of direction
for my highest and best good and
for the good of all.
I trust that God will provide me
with the ideas, motivation, and clarity
for my highest and best manifestation.
I can do anything through my love
and connection to the God source.
The same Infinite Intelligence that
holds the stars in their courses
and maintains the whole universe
in perfect balance keeps me in my
perfect balance now. I dwell in the

security that my needs are met
and that my circumstances are
maintained in perfect balance with
the harmonious whole of life. Order
is the first rule of heaven and my life
is filled with internal motivation,
inspiration and intuition about the
correct direction for me always.
My needs are always met with love.
Love and light always guide me
in all that I do. So be it.

Thank you. Amen.

PRAYER FOR
NEIGHBORLY HARMONY

Dear Infinite Intelligence:
I call on you now to bring peace
and harmony to all neighbors so
we can live happily near each other.
I send love and blessings to all my
neighbors and I ask there be peace,
understanding, and goodwill.
I resist no one and no one resists me.
Nothing from without can disturb me.
There are no troublesome people in my life.
I recognize the God within myself and
recognize the God within everyone else.
I love everyone and everyone loves me
in my neighborhood. I bring love where I go.
I am a peacemaker and I dwell in harmony.
I automatically dissolve any discord

or disagreements between my
neighbors and myself.
I am willing to see the Divine within
them and they see the Divine within me.
Every thought that is not based
on love and harmony now dissolves.
I chose love and harmony in
all areas of my life. So be it.

Thank you. Amen.

PRAYER FOR
OVERCOMING BETRAYAL

Dear Spirit:
Please heal my heart for it is wounded.
I have been betrayed and a bond is broken.
I understand that spirit is my true source
and I am never alone or forsaken.
I am safe in spirit's love and grace.
Thank you for restraining me from
confrontation. Thank you for reminding
me not to take this personally;
this is not really about me.
I can choose to not be offended or hurt,
and that is my power right now.
Thank you, spirit, for helping me
become neutral about this situation.
I ask for my helpers to assist me to
emotionally detach from this and forgive.

I turn over this matter to you, spirit,
and ask for the Christ consciousness
within me work with the
Christ consciousness within them.
All things are healing and released
now and forever. So be it.

Thank you. Amen.

PRAYER FOR
PARTNERSHIP WITH GOD

Dear Infinite Intelligence:
I know that I am one with
the Source of my being.
I am one with all good things
that are coming to me,
and I am one with the good
things I can provide for others.
I bless all who come into my life this day,
pledging myself to provide the highest
service I can to them.
All my relationships respond
to me as a beloved partner,
giving to me as I give to them.
Thank you, my God Source,
for the continuing revelation
of this perfect law in my life.
And so it is.

Thank you. Amen.

PRAYER FOR PEACE

Dear Christ Consciousness:
I ask the Divine Consciousness to now
channel my love energy and the assistance
of my helpers to _____.
I ask that the love and Light
that I am sending goes to _____'s
higher and physical self for
the highest and best good.
The Christ Consciousness within me
Works with the Christ Conscious within

_____.

All things that are out of harmony
are now healed and all negative energy
is released and transformed into
love energy between us.
I send love, appreciation, and gratitude
for the lessons I have learned because

of my connections to _____.
I ask the Christ Consciousness restore
all energy patterns that bring everyone
back into harmony, peace, and love.
Thank you for restoring love back
into our lives and worlds. All is well.
So be it.

Thank you. Amen.

PRAYER FOR
PHYSICAL PROTECTION

Dear Infinite Intelligence:
I know I am always Divinely
protected wherever I am or wherever I go.
I am surrounded by love and light
and all I have to do is be in tune
with my connection to the Infinite
Intelligence for guidance.
I now call on all those who serve and guide
me to point me to safety at all times.
Awaken my intuition and my instincts
to any physical, emotional, mental,
spiritual, or financial danger.
Thank you for the clear signs
around me that alert me to danger.
Awaken me to see deception and
untruth in others and to see the

truth in all situations.
Give me the ability to not react
in situations but to act in accordance
with my truth and for my
protection at all times.
I am calm knowing that wherever
I am and whatever I do,
I am safe in the presence of
Infinite Intelligence. So be it.

Thank you. Amen.

PRAYER FOR PROSPERITY

Dear God:
All my needs are instantaneously
met now and all the days of my life.
Everything I need is provided to me
through the Divine Power
and presence of Infinite Intelligence.
I live in the joyous expectation
of the best from life, and invariably
the best always comes to me. So be it.

Thank you. Amen.

PRAYER FOR RELATIONSHIP HARMONY

Dear Heavenly Mother and Father:
Please bless this relationship that I am in.
Please inspire me to be the highest
and best partner I can be.
Thank you for giving me the ability
to focus in on all the positive
characteristics of my partner and allowing
me to invoke their highest and best.
The wisdom of Infinite Intelligence allows
us to see each other with love and light.
There is harmony, love, peace, and
understanding between us at all times.
So be it.

Thank you. Amen.

PRAYER TO
RELEASE ANXIETY

Dear God:
In the clear bright light of Divine Truth,
there is no darkness or overwhelm.
Nothing troubles me.
I cast all my burdens, anxiety,
and confusion on to the Divine Source
of all love. Love is the law of life.
I sow love into all that I do and
think and feel. I cast all mental troubles
unto the Infinite Intelligence and know
that I can release my worries.
I am transformed into peace.
Please reveal yourself to me
in new ways today.
Fill my heart with your comfort.
Fill my body and mind with your strength.

Help me trade my anxiety,
and stress for peace and order in my life.
I allow the Divine Energy of love
to guide me daily and I dwell
in the kingdom of harmony and order.
I bring love and peace wherever I go.
All is well in my world. I am open to heavenly
inspiration and guidance
for seeing new solutions.
I feel confident that all is well because
the God source is with me at all times.
So be it.

Thank you. Amen.

PRAYER TO
RELEASE CONFLICT

Dear Divine Spirit:
I ask you to hold me and all those souls
that I am in conflict or have difficulty
with, in your healing light.
I ask that you now heal these
relationships now and forever.
Give me the strength to see the
good in these people.
Allow my good thoughts and my love
and my prayers to embody them.
I forgive and release all those who
have ever hurt or offended me.
I now forgive them totally and completely.
Forgiveness opens the door
to divine right action in my reality.
The Christ consciousness within

me works with the Christ
consciousness within them.
And all things are healed
and forgiven forever. So be it.

Thank you. Amen.

PRAYER TO RELEASE
EMOTIONAL STRESS

Dear Infinite Intelligence:
Assist me to remember that
I am connected to source at all times.
I know that to be disturbed about one's
life and affairs, even for an instant,
is not to trust the Divine Love that
is gifted to me daily by the God Source.
I know in my heart that
Infinite Intelligence is taking care of me.
I trust this loving care in all that I do.
If things are stressful, I am not disturbed
because I am one with the love
of the Infinite Intelligence.
I know when things feel out of sorts
that my life and affairs are seeking balance.
I know that my highest and best good

will come into being with my faith
and my connection to the love energy.
Solutions and answers will show up
for me when I trust the power
of the divine love working in my life.
I love the Divine Law of life
and trust in every part of my life.
I am one with and dwell in the
circle of Infinite Intelligence love.
All is well. So be it.

Thank you. Amen.

PRAYER TO
RELEASE GRUDGES

Dear Infinite Intelligence:
I know in my heart it doesn't serve me
to hold a grudge. Any negative thoughts
or energy about a person or situation only
makes that dark energy reflect back to me.
My intellect knows it is not good
to harbor resentful thoughts.
I ask Infinite Intelligence to gently remind
me that to harbor grudges is not in my
best interest and to inspire me to forgive
and release that story from my life.
I choose to release the energy of injustice,
betrayal, and anger that I have been
carrying around. I release victimhood
and I forgive and release all concerned.
I take responsibility in my life for being

part of this drama and I have the power to
stop carrying this baggage around with me.
Today I declare my freedom from this old
burden of regret and grudges.
I no longer have the responsibility
of holding on to these grudges.
I am grateful to let go and regain
my spiritual integrity and
understanding that we are all one.
Souls are on different levels of
consciousness and it is my
responsibility to be a Light Worker.
I leave light, not dark, in the world.
So be it.

Thank you. Amen.

PRAYER TO RELEASE
NEGATIVE ENERGY

Dear Source:
I call on the Divine within myself to
remove all dark energies from people
or situations that are affecting me.
Remove all dark connections from my body,
aura, home, workplace, and vehicles.
I call on the Divine with myself to fill me
and shield me with brilliant Cosmic Light
and create a cocoon of Light around me,
always protecting me from anything
that is not from the light.
I ask that Infinite Intelligence also protect
my family, friends, co-workers, and
neighbors from any dark energy.
I ask the Divine Light within myself
to cleanse, shield, protect, and heal my

connection to the Divine Love and Light
Energy of God at all times.
I am always protected and safe. So be it.

Thank you. Amen.

Prayer to Release Overwhelm & Stress

Dear Cosmic Love Energy:
Solutions and miracles will show up
for me when I trust and accept the power
of the Divine Love working in my life.
I dwell in the circle of
Infinite Intelligence's love.
My awareness of the presence of
this love in my life is my sure defense
against all negative people, situations,
and circumstances. In the clear bright
light of Divine Truth, there is no
darkness or confusion. Nothing
troubles me. Love is the law of life.
I sow love into all that I do, think, and feel.
Where there are troubles I say "peace, be
still." I let go and let God and everything in

my world becomes harmonious. I allow the
divine energy of love to guide me daily and I
dwell in the kingdom of harmony and joy.
I bring love and peace wherever I go.
Infinite Intelligence you carry my
worries away, you transform me,
and you change my heart.
I am strong through my Divine Cosmic
Love connection to you and am not tempted
to take everything into my own hands.
I turn over my challenges to the Divine and
accept that life is a marathon and not a sprint.
All is well. So be it.

Thank you. Amen.

PRAYER TO
RELEASE PROBLEMS

Dear God:
When things go bad, I urgently
need a fresh perspective.
I am releasing this problem to you,
knowing that your Divine Wisdom will bring
the perfect solutions to this situation.
Your Infinite Wisdom knows
the answer to all challenges.
I let go and let God handle this problem
to bring peace, harmony, and well-being
now into my life and all those affected.
I release complaints, victimhood, and all
anger associated with this problem.
I now forgive and release all those
who I have allowed to hurt me in any way.
I am now confident that the perfect solution

will present itself at the perfect time for the highest and best for all concerned.

I face my future with the knowing that I can let go and let God handle whatever I face.

I open my mind to listening to my intuition with an open heart about what actions to take and when. I envision and pray for this problem to dissipate and I trust in God to make that happen. So be it.

Thank you. Amen.

PRAYER TO RELEASE
SITUATIONS & BAD HABITS

Dear Heavenly Mother and Father:
Thank you for inspiring me to have the
courage, insight, strength, and ability
to release all relationships, material objects,
situations, un-resourceful habits, and life
patterns that are no longer to my
highest and best good.
I now allow my soul
to realize its full potential.
I release all need to hold on to
emotions and ideas of lack and limitation
that are connected to the past.
I now forgive everything in the past.
I am, in this moment, creating my future
and I now design my life from a place
of true empowerment.

I unconditionally love and
support myself in all my power
and accept Divine Love in my life.
I am at peace. So be it.

Thank you. Amen.

PRAYER TO RELEASE WHO OR WHAT IS NO LONGER WORKING FOR YOU

Dear God:
Give me the strength and courage to
release relationships, positions, and
environments that are no longer
beneficial to me. I trust my
intuition and inspiration from my
God Source and I know from your
guidance that to attract what I want,
I must release what is not working for me.
Assist me to recognize without anger or
judgment when it is time for me to
let go of the old and create a new reality for
myself that allows all those involved to thrive.
Help me release all concerned with grace,
peace, and harmony. I ask that the release

and parting of ways is mutually beneficial
for all parties. I call upon cosmic
love to heal all concerned. Everyone is
now free to prosper on new paths.
The wisdom of Infinite Intelligence now
assists all concerned to see each other with
harmony, love, peace, and understanding.
I am now attracting new Energy and Light
that will assist me to prosper
in all aspects of my life.
I am enjoying new relationships, positions,
and environments, and opportunities
flow to me now easily and effortlessly.
I always trust I am connected
to the God Source. I am always
receiving guidance on what directions
to take in my life. So be it.

Thank you. Amen.

PRAYER TO
RELEASE WORRY

Dear Creator:
When I worry, I lose my connection to you.
Thank you for opening my mind and heart to
the knowledge that my connection to you,
the Creator, will transcend all worldly
doubts, fears, and worries.
I accept the truth that worry is impotent
to change tomorrow or redo the past.
Worry depletes me and blocks inspiration
from the Infinite Intelligence
on how to solve any situation.
I call upon you to help me overcome all
worries, anxieties, and fear thought patterns.
Grant me the courage and strength
to surrender these destructive thoughts

to you and set me free.
All that I need flows to me
through the power of the Creator.
I know in my heart that
nothing is impossible.
I now allow new solutions to come
to me through an open heart and mind.
I let the Creator express through me
as Divine right action. I now surrender
all my worries to you. Thank you for releasing
me from the prison of worry
and into the joy of a new day and life.
A new, free life awaits me. So be it.

Thank you. Amen.

Prayer to Relieve Depression

Dear Divine Source:
Give me the insight to see that this, too,
shall pass and understand that these
feelings of depression and hopelessness
are temporary. I am loving and kind to
myself. I give myself permission to move
past these temporary feelings of depression.
I am never separated from the Cosmic Force
of Love even when I feel depressed or blue.
I have the power within me to connect
to your Source and see the blessings
and good in my life.
I know that your power is within me,
for I am the perfect Child of God.
I accept the good in my life now; I am healed.
I am blessed, protected, and loved.

In your name I command the depression
within me now to be banished, and
to be replaced with thoughts of
gratitude and love for Source.
I open my heart and mind to you,
Dear Source, for my good.
All is well and always will be well.
Good now comes to me. So be it.

Thank you. Amen.

PRAYER TO
RELIEVE OVERWORK

Dear Lord:
I ask for your help now to release
the burdens I feel about my work.
Give me the strength and wisdom
to know when things are my job and
when they are your job.
Allow me to release responsibilities
That are not mine so that I can balance
my life out perfectly.
I know that my burdens
are my own making.
I have taken on these burdens
and responsibilities and I ask now
that those responsibilities that are not
mine be returned to their rightful owners.
I ask for your help in giving
me the ability to plan my work with

more boundaries and time schedules that
protect me from overwork and mental
and physical exhaustion.
Lord, keep me from accepting too
much work for money or prestige
and help me create balance in
my personal and spiritual life.
I attract only the best people, vendors,
and services that bring joy and
ease to my work. I now stop trying to do
everything myself. I ask for my
spiritual helpers on a daily basis
to assist me in my work life.
Bring me out of the darkness into
the light of my place in the world.
Refresh my mental attitudes to accept
that everything has a time and place.
Assist me to bring love of my
work back into my life.
I now release all things that are
no longer beneficial to me. So be it.

Thank you. Amen.

PRAYER FOR RESILIENCY

Mother, Father of the Universe:
Assist me not to take personally
what others say and do.
Open my eyes to the reality that
People have their own past
programming and agendas.
Their perception of life that
has nothing to do with me.
During stressful situations or
people's misbehavior, give me
the awareness to recognize when
others are being unconscious.
Remind me of my choice to be an
observer of the situation and provide
spiritual insight to not take it personally.
Inspire me to act with the awareness
that I co-create my reality with source.
Universe, please give me the strength

to not let old behavior patterns and
wounds within myself be triggered.
Remind me that I am always connected
to the Source and always have
spiritual helpers when I request them.
Thank you for always being with me,
the love connection and understanding
that all is well. Thank you for the
knowledge that I am always taken care
of and that my true important
relationship is with source.
I joyfully forgive all those situations and
people I have allowed to cause me pain.
I release the pain for I now dwell
in the realm of love. I accept and know
that as I shift and change, I will see
others change for the highest and best
good for all concerned.
Thank you for harmony
and peace in all aspects of my life.
I love myself and I am always
connected to source. So be it.

Thank you. Amen.

PRAYER FOR
SAYING GOODBYE

Dear Infinite Intelligence:
I ask that you ease the difficulty of saying
goodbye to the acquaintances, business
associates, friends, and family from
whom I part during this time of separation.
I know that people are drawn together
For mutual growth and sometimes part
under less-than-desirable circumstances.
I accept this truth and now ask Divine
Intelligence to take over and create peace,
love, and harmony in our parting ways.
I trust that by turning over this situation
of saying goodbye that all parties are
blessed and thrive in their new lives.
I feel blessed to know that Divine
Intelligence is within me and is able

to look ahead and plan for my
tomorrows with the right people.
I know that I am in the right place
doing the right things at all times
when I listen to my inner God Self.
I ask the Law of Divine Adjustment
bring my life into balance and I declare
that the powerful law of adjustment is
always operating in my life,
both personally and professionally.
Each relationship in my life
is an opportunity to gain in spiritual
understanding. I send only love, harmony,
blessings, and peace to those I now
say goodbye to. So be it.

Thank you. Amen.

PRAYER FOR
SELF-CONFIDENCE

Dear Source:
I accept without question that
Infinite Intelligence is ever present,
always available. I accept that the wisdom,
intelligence, and power of the Divine
Universe are always at my disposal.
I acknowledge that I have the power to
tap into this unlimited power at any time.
I accept that the answers to all my challenges
and insecurities do not just lie in God's
willingness but in my ability to believe
that I am connected to all that there is.
I am a perfect child of God.
I am the spirit of truth.
With that truth, I can solve any problem
and overcome any difficulty.

Spirit knows no obstruction.
I am always equal to any task set
Before me because I am connected to the
all and I have resources in the invisible
world to connect to daily.
Therefore, I am always confident that
I have the power to meet all challenges.
So be it.

Thank you. Amen.

PRAYER TO
SELL YOUR HOME

Dear Universe:
Surround My Home and property now
with the pure energy of blessings and love.
I know there is a true and perfect buyer
in the world right now looking for this home.
Thank you Universe for arranging the
perfect buyer for this home. Thank you
Universe for orchestrating and supplying
the support, collaboration, and cooperation
from all parties to make the closing
transaction fast and smooth. Allow all those
involved to feel happy and blessed from
this real estate transaction. I pray for the
new buyer to benefit physically, mentally,
spiritually, emotionally, and financially
from their investment of this home.

Thank you Universe for the attraction
of the Divine right buyer at the perfect time.
Thank you for creating a blessed real estate
transaction where everyone wins. So be it.

Thank you. Amen.

PRAYER TO STOP
FINANCIAL STRUGGLE

Dear Creator:
I ask to strengthen our connection,
so that I'm confident and trust that you
are always with me. I ask for you to
inspire me to ask for help early
and often and recognize that I cannot
see the entire picture of my life.
I request that you aid me with Helpers
who can come in the form of other
people's sound advice and counsel,
synchronicity, and new knowledge from
the Creator energy that opens
for my financial wellbeing.
I am now surrendering my financial
affairs to your Divine Love and Care.
I ask that you remove my worries,

anxieties, and fears about money.
I trust that if I listen to my guidance
from you that I will be inspired
with ideas and actions to provide
for myself and my family.
I now release fears, doubts, and all
negative beliefs and thoughts about
my ability to enjoy prosperity and money.
I joyfully commit to learning more
about managing my finances wisely.
I now seek help when required.
I continually ask for your assistance
to match my talents, abilities,
and knowledge with the perfect
clients or customers who will benefit
from my life energy. I ask that there is
always a fair exchange for value between me
and all people where money is concerned.
Thank you for giving me the confidence
and courage to price my services for what they
are worth. I am always living in

a prosperous state of mind.
Money flows to me continually
with ease and joy from positive sources.
All I want and need is supplied to me
from Creator. So be it.

Thank you. Amen.

PRAYER FOR STRENGTH
TO FACE A DIFFICULT TASK

Dear Divine Source of all:
I know I have a challenge in front of me.
I know I dwell in the light and there is no
darkness in my life. I am now willing and
ready for the light to shine and illuminate
the correct path for me to take.
I call to all those who help me now to
lighten my burden by giving me the strength
and courage to face any situation.
Give me intuition and guidance to approach
my challenges in the best way possible.
Inspire me with new viewpoints and the
knowledge that I am never alone on Earth.
I have helpers and guidance that I can feel
and hear when I am calm. I ask that my
negative imagination of all that can go wrong

be replaced with new ideas,
new perspectives, and new support
to be able to handle whatever difficulties I
now face. I acknowledge that I have
the love of the Universe on my side I pay
attention to the small whispers of help that
come to me when I am centered and in
communication with my source of love.
I fear nothing because I am part of the
Divine Source and I am always loved.
So be it.

Thank you. Amen.

Prayer for Studying to Pass a Test or Course

Dear Infinite Intelligence:
Please inspire me and lead me
in my studies and actions.
Help me to easily and effortlessly pass
all my examinations in Divine Order.
I radiate love and goodwill
to all my teachers and classmates.
I am happy, content, and free.
Only good comes from my studies.
So be it.

Thank you. Amen.

PRAYER FOR
UNDERSTANDING

Dear Heavenly Mother and Father:
Please walk through my house and take
away all worries, sadness, financial stress,
and illness. Please watch over and heal
my family, friends, and loved ones.
Please bring quiet and peace where
there is chaos; bring light and love where
there is darkness, and put love in our
hearts. Spirit, assist me to look beyond
circumstances and instead, allow us
to look into each other's hearts to understand
the unique challenges we all face.
Please give me the ability to be
non-judgmental and have more love,
patience, and tolerance for everyone.
And so it is.

Thank you. Amen.

PRAYER FOR
VISIONARY INSIGHT

Dear Heavenly Mother and Father:
Guide me today to delicately steer my
thoughts and images in my mind's eye
to those which are aligned
with my Divine Purpose.
Allow me to be inspired to create
peace, harmony, perfect health,
happiness, prosperity, love,
and well-being in my life.
Assist me to see myself as one
who is filled with vitality, good health,
confidence, creativity, and
enthusiasm for my life and work.
Allow me to work out any "challenges"
in the workshop of my mind
and to see the perfect solutions

as they come to me through intuition.
Thank you for my daily guidance and
for always leading me to my
highest and best good. So be it.

Thank you. Amen.

Prayer for Wealth

Dear Infinite Intelligence:
Wealth is circulating in my life now.
Wealth easily and effortlessly flows
to me in avalanches of abundance.
All my needs, desires, and goals
are met instantaneously.
I am one with Infinite Intelligence
and Infinite Love is everything.
Everything I want and need easily
and effortlessly comes to me
now through God's laws of action.
Large sums of money and prosperity
flow to me now from Divine Order.
So be it.

Thank you. Amen.

Prayer for Wisdom

Mother, Father, God of the Universe:
Divine wisdom is my birthright
and I know to listen to your loving
messages everyday so my mind
is filled with love, harmony,
creativity, insight, and
clear direction for my life.
I pray to you to show me exactly
what I need to know each day.
I am inspired by your
loving guidance and presence.
I am motivated by love and
only speak and act when I am feeling
your guidance. My earthly job is to
bring wisdom, healing, and love into the
world with my thoughts and actions.
I let go of the fears, resentment,

pettiness, and old programming
of confusion and victimhood.
Your wisdom and presence
sustains me through the day.
You provide me strength for this day,
guidance in all my decisions, vision
of the way, courage in adversity,
help from above, and unfailing
empathy and wisdom.
All is well in my life and future.
So be it.

Thank you. Amen.

PRAYER FOR
WORLD HEALING

Dear Infinite Intelligence:
I ask for world healing
and peace where possible.
There is no power in conditions
or situations and there is only
power in the Infinite Intelligence.
Allow me to be a light in the world.
I give up judgment, fault-finding,
and egotistic behavior and look
for the God within all souls.
I accept that I am a spirit
living in an earthly environment.
Inspire me daily to model love,
understanding, and peace to the world.
I know that all things are possible
with God through me and my

actions, thoughts, and beliefs.
I dwell in a circle of love and
nothing but love can enter that circle.
There is no darkness, only
misunderstandings, and I do not
give or receive offense in any way.
Love is the law and purpose of my life.
I declare peace all around me. So be it.

Thank you. Amen.

About Lee Milteer

LEE MILTEER is an internationally known and celebrated bestselling author, award-winning professional speaker, TV personality, entrepreneur, visionary, and intuitive business mentor. In her career, Lee Milteer has shared the platform with many well-known and famous personalities within the spiritual community such as: Deepak Chopra, Tony Robbins, Jack Canfield and Mark Victor Hansen (Chicken Soup for the Soul), Rabbi Daniel Lapin, Shirley MacLaine, T. Harv Eker, John Bradshaw, the late Dr. Norman Vincent Peale, the late Zig Ziglar, and the late Og Mandino. Lee is a rare soul who lives and thrives in both the business world and the metaphysical world.

Lee has been an expert guest on more than 700 TV and radio shows on national and international TV and radio around the world. Lee has been interviewed in newspapers, magazines, and trade journals including *U.S.A. Today*, *Wall Street Journal*, *INC* magazine, and *Glamour*. Lee has had two TV shows in Virginia and worked in Canadian television.

Lee has created and hosted educational programs airing on PBS and other cable networks throughout the U.S. and Canada. She is the author of the books *Success Is an Inside Job* and *Spiritual Power Tools*, as well as the co-author of ten books. Lee's eleventh book, *Reclaim the Magic*, was released in May 2015 and became an instant best seller on Amazon.

Lee speaks all over the world and has counseled and trained over one million people in her speeches. Lee has authored over 150 training, entrepreneurial, spiritual, and educational products. She is the founder of the Millionaire Smarts® Coaching program, in which she provides success and spiritual advice and resources to people worldwide. Lee also runs coaching programs to help people use their potential and purpose in the business world and personal life.

In recognition of her achievements, Lee Milteer was awarded the title of Dame (Lady) of the Order of the Imperial and Charitable Order of Constantine the Great and Saint Helen (one of the oldest Orders of Knighthood in the world). Lee was also honored for her contribution to humankind, human values, and quality of character.

Lee has spoken and given seminars at Edgar Cayce's Association for Research and Enlightenment (A.R.E.), and personally worked with Robert Monroe from the Monroe Institute (which provides experiential education programs facilitating the personal exploration of human consciousness).

Lee has studied in Mystery Schools, the Rosicrucian Order, and with many private shamans, healers, and professional psychics. Lee herself is also a Reiki Healer, runs a Mystery School, and offers many resources on how to successfully live both in the spiritual and mainstream worlds. Lee is a philanthropist and works with SPCA and other animal rescue organizations to raise money and awareness for animals.

Lee is not only an extraordinarily successful businesswoman and metaphysician, she is also a talented artist, writer, photographer, and painter.

Lee lives in Virginia Beach, Virginia on the Chesapeake Bay on the beach with her animal companions, and her husband Clifton.

Free Resources
from Lee Milteer

THE FIVE TYPES OF
ENERGY VIDEO SERIES

Instead of letting the world control you, decide how you will use your Life Energy! I am going to gift you my entire 5-Video Series (a $97 Value) on How to Manage Your Financial, Mental, Emotional, Physical, and Spiritual Life Energy Currencies.

To find out more about your five types of energy and how to more effectively use them in your life, sign up for my free video series. Go to *www.fivetypesofenergy.com* today!

SPIRITUAL POWER TOOLS
FOR PROFIT AND PURPOSE E-ZINE

Looking for practical and spiritual solutions to life's challenges? Go to *www.spritiualpowertools.com* and sign up for my free weekly e-zine, *Spiritual*

Power Tools for Profit and Purpose, where I share time-tested, spiritually-based strategies for conquering challenges, overcoming obstacles, and succeeding in this adventure called life!

Be sure to visit Lee Milteer at: *www.leemilteerschoolofwisdom.com* for more information on her books, courses, special events, vision quests, and Mystery School classes.

Mystery Schools began in ancient times and are vehicles for the transmission of spiritual wisdom and open to all light workers and seekers of the truth.

Lee has studied in metaphysical mystery schools and with spiritual masters all of her life. She provides you with secret teachings and trainings that, when practiced correctly, allow you to go beyond normal realities and manifest the true power that the Universe has given you.

www.leemilteerschoolofwisdom.com/mysteryschool.php

Related Titles

If you enjoyed *The Magic of Prayers,* you may also enjoy other Rainbow Ridge titles. Read more about them at *www.rainbowridgebooks.com.*

God's Message to the World: You've Got Me All Wrong
by Neale Donald Walsch

The Secret of Effortless Being
by Ronny Hatchwell and Zach Sivan

Rita's World
by Frank DeMarco

Soul Courage
by Tara-jenelle Walsch

Quantum Economics
by Amit Goswami

Coming Full Circle:
Ancient Teachings for a Modern World
by Lynn Andrews

*Consciousness: Bridging the Gap Between Conventional
Science and the New Super Science of Quantum Mechanics* by
Eva Herr

Messiah's Handbook: Reminders for the Advanced Soul
by Richard Bach

Blue Sky, White Clouds
by Eliezer Sobel

Inner Vegas: Creating Miracles Abundance, and Health
by Joe Gallenberger

*Your Soul Remembers: Accessing
Your Past Lives through Soul Writing*
by Joanne DiMaggio

Rainbow Ridge Books publishes spiritual, metaphysical,
and self-help titles, and is distributed by Square One
Publishers in Garden City Park, New York.

To contact authors and editors, peruse our titles, and see
submission guidelines, please visit our website at
www.rainbowridgebooks.com.